T0132454

Suctioncup

By Brian Cook

WestBow Press books may be ordered through booksellers or by contacting:

WestBow Press
A Division of Thomas Nelson & Zondervan
1663 Liberty Drive
Bloomington, IN 47403
www.westbowpress.com
844-714-3454

ISBN: 979-8-3850-0169-9 (sc)
ISBN: 979-8-3850-0171-2 (e)

Library of Congress Control Number: 2023911923

Print information available on the last page.

WestBow Press rev. date: 10/11/2023

WESTBOW
PRESS®
A DIVISION OF THOMAS NELSON
& ZONDERVAN

This is Carter and Cooper.

They think fishing is super!

They grab their poles
and fishing gear,

And walk to the pond, by their
house, that's near.

Their dad puts the worms on their hooks as bait.

4

They cast out their lines
and patiently wait.

When their bobbers
go under, they shout
out with glee,

"This one's a bass.... I know it, you'll see!"

Carter cranked his reel
once the hook he did set,

"Cooper," said Carter,
"Quickly grab me the net!"

8

They posed for a picture with the bass they'd just caught,

For bass was the kind of fish they all sought.

"OK," said their dad,
"Tell the bass goodbye."

"It's time it went back in
the water nearby"

Then Carter grabbed
the net, to be ready
for another,

When in it he saw a
creature like no other,

12

"What is it?" asked Carter as he stared at the thing,

"Can we keep it," asked the
boys, "until it's a frog?"

"You mean like a pet," Dad said,
"Like Roxie our dog?"

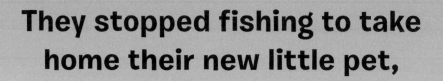

They stopped fishing to take
home their new little pet,

To show to their mommy what
they caught in their net.

16

When she saw it she asked, "Did you give it a name?"
Carter thought for a moment and then he proclaimed,
"Suctioncup," he shouted, "will be his new name!"
He asked his mommy, "Can we keep him for good?"
She said with a smile, "For one night we sure could."

That night when the boys were lying in bed,

Mommy heard Carter pray to God when he said,

"Lord, keep Suctioncup healthy and strong."

"So he'll be our pet and to our family belong."

His prayer brought a tear to his mommy's eye.

"Now we must keep him," she smiled and sighed.

The next morning their mommy announced to the boys, "We're keeping Suctioncup for all to enjoy!" "But only until he's grown and become, the frog we all want him to be and then some"

20

The boys ran and hugged their mommy so tight, "Thank you thank you!" they screamed with the utmost delight

Each morning, when Carter first woke up,

He ran to the tank
where they kept
Suctioncup.

He watched him change
and start to grow,

"How big would he get?"
Carter wanted to know.

His tail grew longer and
his body got bigger,

"*What was next,*"
thought Carter, he just
couldn't figure?

His tail started shrinking,
and his legs did appear,

"He's becoming a frog!" Carter
shouted and cheered.

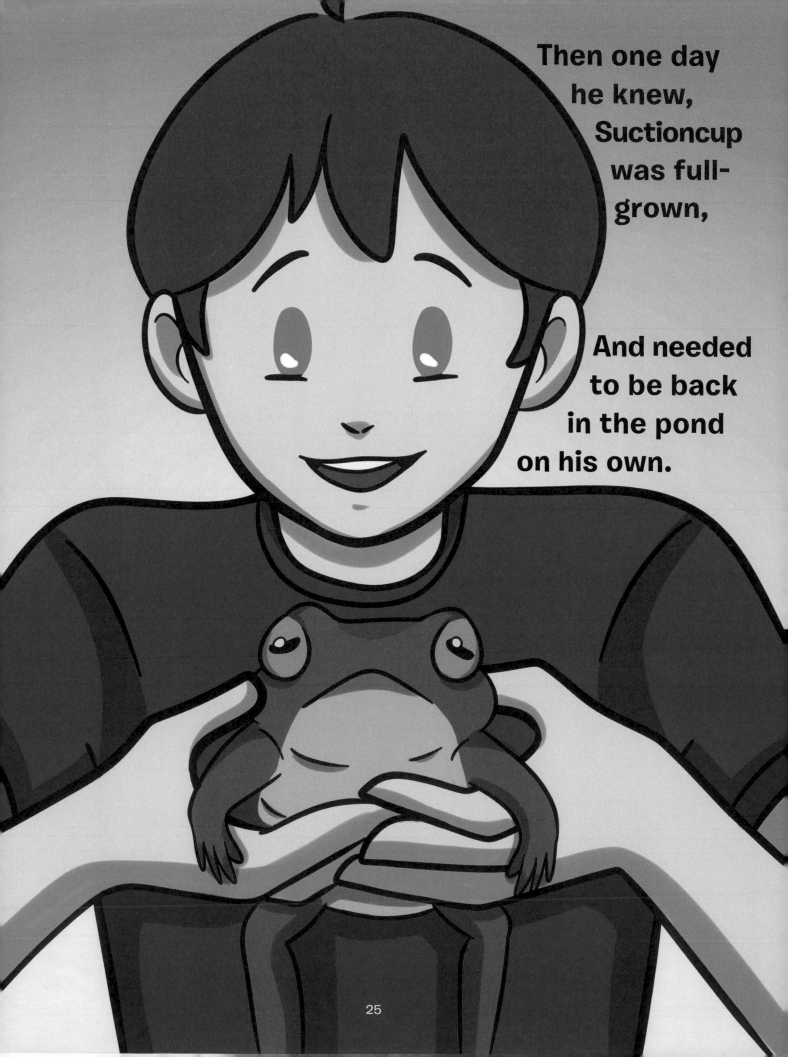

Then one day he knew, Suctioncup was full-grown,

And needed to be back in the pond on his own.

25

So Carter and Cooper, with their mommy and daddy,
took Suctioncup back to the pond to be happy.

Before putting him in Carter quietly said,
"Be happy and safe my little frog friend."

Then into the
water, Suctioncup
he did send.

The End